The Advent Jesse Tree

Mary Nel
1989

The Advent Jesse Tree

Devotions
for
Children and Adults
to prepare for the coming
of the
CHRIST CHILD
at
CHRISTMAS

Dean Meador Lambert

Illustrations by Ginger Meador

Abingdon Press
Nashville

DEDICATION

To My Family
and
My Church—
From their "roots"
My Love for
the Lord has grown.

ISBN 0-687-00908-1
First printing, November, 1988
Second printing, September, 1989
Third printing 1990

Manufactured in the United States of America

Credits are on page 96.

CONTENTS

Several years ago a women's group in my church decided to create an Advent Jesse Tree for the Christmas season as a fundraising project for missions. We made ornaments to trace the heritage of Jesus Christ, and I was in charge of preparing devotions which coincided with these ornaments.

As I began researching in preparation for this project, I realized that an old idea of a Jesse Tree could make the Advent season become one of the most meaningful times of the year for my children and family. I wanted the *Advent Jesse Tree* to not only teach about the roots of our Lord but to provide a time when we as a family could prepare our hearts and lives for the birthday of Christ.

When writing the devotions, I remembered a phrase that I once heard: "The Old Testament conceals what the New Testament reveals." I realized that this statement could be the purpose of these devotions. What was the Old Testament concealing? How are so many events and people in these sacred Books of the Word tied together? What do they have in common?

The answers to these questions are revealed in the very first chapter of the New Testament, where it is written that a tiny, unpretentious baby was born. The 21st verse says, "And she shall bring forth a son, and thou shalt call his name Jesus for he shall save his people from their sins." This was the purpose of the Old Testament! God chose a people to bring forth His only Son. Although these chosen people would not understand many of the events God would allow to happen to them, His purpose would finally be revealed when Jesus came to earth.

During the Advent season each year, it is important to remember not only the sentimental story, but the powerful meaning of Christmas. The plan of salvation did not start with the birth of a tiny baby in the lowliest of places. The preincarnate Christ was present before the beginning. The history of the Old Testament sets the stage for this babe born at Christmas who would perform the work of salvation for us on the Cross. This powerful message is what the Advent Jesse Tree seeks to reveal.

Each Christmas my family looks forward to this special time of devotions. From the youngest to the eldest, each child anticipates her turn to open the ornament for the day and hang it on our "special" Christmas tree. The hustle and bustle the world teaches at Christmas is slowly silenced as the Bible is opened and the story is read. It is exciting to see how the stories and prophecies "concealed" are slowly "revealed" to us in new insights gained from the Scriptures. As the family sings the hymns around the piano or softly whispers a prayer in song, we begin eagerly awaiting the birth of the Christ Child.

My prayer is that this devotional book will be just as meaningful to you as it has been to my family. Please share in the power of the Advent season as day by day we eagerly prepare our hearts and lives for the coming Savior.

DEAN M. LAMBERT
Hattiesburg, Mississippi

What Is the
Advent Jesse Tree?

The word *Advent* means "coming" and refers to the coming of Jesus. The Advent Jesse Tree emphasizes His coming in the flesh at Bethlehem nearly two thousand years ago. It also explains His coming with the New Covenant and His second coming when He will return to judge all of mankind. The Advent season is a time for all of us to prepare for these "comings."

The Advent Jesse Tree seeks to tell the story of God's redemptive plan for the world through 25 symbols from the Old and New Testament. The symbols trace the heritage of Jesus Christ from the beginning of creation. Each symbol is explained with scriptures, devotions, questions, prayers, a memory verse, and songs. Use the devotions and symbols in this book for your Advent quiet time. You may choose to make ornaments and place them on a small Christmas tree to coincide with this book of symbols.

The first symbol takes us back to Christ's pre-existence before all of creation. The second and third symbols show the beginning of sin, the need for a Savior, and the covenantal promise of God to redeem us.

Symbols 4 through 9 portray the establishment of this covenant with a chosen people who would be the example of ones blessed by God. Through these chosen people of God, One would come to fulfill the beautiful covenant from God. The symbols of the lamb and the ladder are a prefiguration of Christ and His death on Calvary.

The symbol of Ruth, symbol number 10, shows

God's plan of salvation reaching beyond the Jewish race to include all people who trust in Him. In Matthew, Ruth is listed an ancestress of Christ and brings us as Gentiles into His lineage.

Symbols number 12 and 13 bring us back to the Jewish race with King David and King Josiah. Although many years and many kings passed between these symbols, it is apparent that God never forgot His promise to bring a greater King to the world through the royal lineage of the Jewish nation.

Following Solomon's reign as King, the Jewish nation became two countries, Israel and Judah. As a result of many years of disobedience, God sent His people into exile. Just prior to and during the time of exile, prophets arose proclaiming the coming of the Messiah. Symbols number 13 through 19 are prophecies foretelling certain characteristics or events concerning the "new shoot" from the stump of Jesse. The little town of Bethlehem would bring forth a King, Prince of Peace, Shepherd, and Suffering Servant to write a new covenant on the hearts of all who believe in Him.

Symbols number 20 and 21 show clearly the presence of God with His people in exile, in the return, and in all times of suffering. Nearly 400 years would pass before the New Testament would begin with the birth of the Messiah. The Christmas Story begins to unfold with symbols number 22 through 24 and then on Christmas Day, symbol number 25, our Emmanuel comes to bless and to save all who will worship Him at the manger.

How to Use Your
Advent Jesse Tree

The Advent Jesse Tree book is designed for its use alone in a meaningful devotional experience. The symbols in this book beautifully portray the heritage of Christ.

You may choose, however, to use a small tree with ornaments to coincide with the book. Here are some suggestions in preparing this tree: First, choose a shapely tree branch, real or artificial, two or three feet in height. Place it in a pot of earth, and cover the pot with bright paper. You may wish to use a small artificial Christmas tree which may be used year after year during the Advent season.

Make or purchase an ornament for each day--25 in all. Wrap them individually and place them under your Advent Jesse Tree. Although Advent season traditionally begins in November each year, the devotions begin on the first day of December and end on Christmas Day. The ornaments should be used with these devotions, opening one ornament each day, placing it on the tree, and sharing a devotion together. On page 12 is a list of suggestions for your ornaments or symbols.

If you are unable to make or buy your ornaments, you are encouraged to be creative with your own ideas. One family has used pictures cut from magazines as their special ornaments. Some children have painted or created their own designs. Nevertheless, other families choose to use the illustrations of the symbols found in this book as the primary source to coincide with their devotions. Permission is given to copy these illustrations to use as ornaments for your tree.

Many people go to great lengths to prepare for Christmas, yet fail to appreciate the true meaning of the Advent season. If properly used, "The Advent Jesse Tree" will help you and your family to more completely understand the coming of Christ.

Symbols or Ornaments
for the Advent Jesse Tree

1. a globe or picture of the earth
2. an apple and a snake wrapped around it
3. an ark with a rainbow
4. a camel and a tent
5. a lamb
6. a ladder
7. a colorful coat
8. a tablet with ten numbers
9. a cluster of grapes
10. a sheaf of wheat
11. a slingshot
12. a scroll or Bible
13. a stump with fresh shoot or green leaf
14. a lion and a lamb
15. a dove and a crown
16. a lamb and a shepherd's staff
17. a cross
18. a heart with writing on it
19. a Bethlehem town silhouette with star
20. a fiery furnace
21. a brick wall
22. a star
23. a candle or light
24. an angel
25. a baby in a manger or a nativity scene

DAY ONE

The Light in Creation

Symbol: a globe or picture of the Earth

Memory Verse: "In the beginning, God created the heavens and the earth." GENESIS 1:1

Hymns to Sing:
  "He's Got the Whole World in His Hands"
  "All Things Bright and Beautiful"
  "How Great Thou Art"
  "This Is My Father's World"

THE LIGHT IN CREATION

(CHILDREN)

Scriptures: Genesis 1:1 and John 1:1-4

Devotion: Did you see something wonderful to-day? (Name some things.) The big round world that we live on is wonderful. (Show symbol) Do you know who made that world and everything around us? (God) Let's look in our Bible and see. (Read Genesis 1:1)

Before that beginning there was no round world. In fact, the world was once as dark as night, and you couldn't see anything. But God was there. He has always been, and when God said, "Let there be light," there was light!

Did you know that Jesus was there with God when the world was made? Let's look again in our Bible. (John 1:1-4) Jesus is our Light. There was light in the world so we could know Him and love Him and praise Him!

After He made the beautiful earth, God made a man named Adam and a woman named Eve. They lived in a beautiful garden with all the animals. When God looked at all He had created, He thought everything was *very good!*

Questions:
"What did the world look like in the beginning?"
 (no animals, seas, darkness, etc.)
"Was God there in the darkness?"
"Who made the world, Adam and Eve, and
 everything?"
"Who is our Light?"

Prayer: Father in Heaven, we belong to Thee because You made us and our world. We thank You for creating such a beautiful place for us to live.

14

Most of all we thank You for Jesus, who was born a little baby to be our Light of the World so we could know and love You. Amen. (Would you like to thank Him for some things He has made for you?)

THE LIGHT IN CREATION

(ADULTS)

Scriptures: Genesis 1 and 2; John 1:1-4, 17:5, 24; Colossians 1:16, 17; Psalm 150

Devotion: In Genesis One, we have the first teaching of the Trinity with God the Father, God the Son, and God the Holy Spirit all being a part of the Creation. This is made more evident to us as the scriptures above reveal. We can also apply the creation story to our lives spiritually. Outside of God, life has no purpose. We are in darkness. The Light comes when we give ourselves to Christ. Our lives now become meaningful because we have found our purpose--to glorify Him!

Prayer: Thank You God for Your beautiful world. Thank You for each person You have created in Your image. Most of all we thank You for Jesus, our Light and Life. Help us to rejoice in Your creation. May we never take advantage of the resources You have given us. Help us to be wise caretakers of Your world, eager to show Your Light through our lives with all people. Amen.

DAY TWO

The First Sin

Symbol: an apple and a snake wrapped around it

Memory Verse: "All we like sheep have gone astray;
we have turned everyone to his own way."
ISAIAH 53:6

Hymns to Sing:
"Jesus Loves Me"
"Love Divine, All Loves Excelling"
"Just as I Am"

THE FIRST SIN

(CHILDREN)

Scriptures: Genesis 3:1-10, 23; Isaiah 53:6

Devotion: When God first made the world He saw that everything was good, but now there are bad things in the world. Can you think of some bad things? (killing, being ugly, talking bad, etc.) Do you know how these bad things got into God's beautiful world? It was because of sin. Sin is not doing what God wants you to do, and the Bible says that Satan came into the world to make us turn away from God.

Do you know who Satan is? One of his names is the Devil, and he hates God and wants everyone else to hate God too. In the beginning Satan saw that the most wonderful of all God's works were Adam and Eve. He set out to make them disobey God. Do you know how he did it?

(Show symbol) He went into the beautiful garden where they were living and dressed up like a snake. There was one tree of fruit God had told Adam and Eve not to eat, and if they did, He had told them they would die. Satan came to Eve and lied to her. He told her she would not die, but instead she would be just like God. Eve listened to the lies of Satan. In fact, she and Adam both ate of the forbidden fruit!

Adam and Eve did what Satan wanted them to do. They disobeyed God and became sinners. Did they die? Their bodies did not die, but they would die in another way. They could not talk or walk with God. They were not able to live with Him in the garden. He sent them out to work and when they got old, their bodies then died.

The only way to get back to God was to take sin away. When all seemed hopeless, God found a Way for us to come back to Him. That very day God promised a Savior, Jesus, who would come and take sin away and bring us back to God. God loves us very much!

Questions:
"What is sin?" (Not doing what God tells us to do)
"Who is Satan?"
"How did Adam and Eve sin?"
"Are we sinners?" (Isaiah 53:6)
"How do we know God still loves us?" (He sent us Jesus)

Prayer: Dear God, we are so sorry we do wrong things. Just as Adam and Eve sinned, we are sinning every day. Help us to do what is right. Thank You for sending Jesus to us so our sins could be forgiven. Because of Your Love, we can now live close to You. Amen.

THE FIRST SIN
(ADULTS)

Scriptures: Genesis 3; 1 John 1:8-10; Isaiah 59:2; 53:6

Devotion: Recorded in Genesis is the beginning of sin, but also we see the first chapters in the history of God's redemptive plan. This is the substance of the whole Bible. From the beginning, humans have sought to exalt their own will above God's will. Yet God is eternally calling us to be with Him through His Son Jesus Christ. In Genesis 3:15, we have the promise of redemption for the sins of all of us. Today we can see this in the first promise of a Savior to come, foretelling the sufferings of Christ and the final victory over His enemy Satan. The Seed of the woman would crush the Serpent!

Prayer: We are sinful, O God. Keep us mindful that apart from You we are nothing. Thank You for loving us even in our sin and for providing a Way to be with You again. Teach us to watch over one another in love through Your Son, Jesus Christ. Amen.

DAY THREE

Inside the Ark

Symbol: an ark with a rainbow

Memory Verse: "For the wages of sin is death; but the gift of God is eternal life through Jesus Christ our Lord." ROMANS 6:23

Hymns to Sing:
  "Arky, Arky"
  "Standing on the Promises"

INSIDE THE ARK

(CHILDREN)

Scriptures: Genesis 6:5-8; 7:17-23; 9:16; Romans 6:23

Devotion: Do you remember how Adam and Eve sinned and were sent out from the garden to work? After that, sin grew worse and worse. Soon there were many people who did not love God, and they were doing things God did not want them to do. This made God very unhappy! He decided to destroy all the bad people by sending a great flood! There was one man, however, who did love God and followed Him in all His ways. Do you remember his name? (Noah)

God told Noah to build an ark, which is a very big boat. If Noah was faithful, God would save his family. Sure enough, the flood came, and all the people outside the boat were drowned. Only those in the ark were saved.

Do you think you should be punished if you sin? Let's read what the Bible says about sin. (Romans 6:23) Those who do not turn to God will be lost forever, just like the people outside the ark, but God promised us life if we are *in* Jesus!

Do you remember what God used to show Noah He would always keep His promises? (rainbow) Whenever we see a rainbow, we will remember that God loves us and He keeps His promises! One of His promises is to give us Life forever in Jesus!

Questions:
"Why did God tell Noah to build a boat?"
"What happened to those who did not love God?"
"What will happen to us if we sin?"
"What does He promise us, if we love Him?"
"Does God keep His promises?"

Prayer: Dear Lord, we know we do bad things and deserve to be punished just like the wicked people of Noah's day. But we are so glad You promised to forgive our sins if we believe *in* Jesus. Thank You for the rainbow with its beautiful colors, and thank You that You keep all Your promises. In Jesus' name. Amen.

INSIDE THE ARK

(ADULTS)

Scriptures: Genesis 5-9:17; Romans 6:23; Joshua 23:14

Devotion: For thousands of years people had existed. The evil in man's nature had taken over and they had rejected God. The great catastrophe of the Flood was used as a means of judgment.

The ark was Noah's salvation just as Jesus is our ark. In Him alone can we be saved. In verse 14 of Genesis 6 the word "pitch" in the Hebrew literally means "atonement." The ark is the clearest type in the Old Testament of the believer's salvation found in Jesus Christ. A "type" is defined as a person, object, or event in the Old Testament regarded as foreshadowing a corresponding reality of the New Law in Christ. After the ark was completed, man was invited to enter. Jesus says, "Come unto Me." It is an invitation, not a command.

We then see the rainbow-symbol of a covenant between God and man. Promises are made by God and are eternal. They are always full of grace. We have the rainbow preaching the fact that for the sake of redemption the world is spared.

Prayer: Holy Lord God, we know we have grieved You many times by our selfishness and sin. We deserve destruction, but You have promised us salvation through Your Son Jesus Christ. You even count us worthy to enter into a covenant with You. You have given us a reminder of Yourself, not in the furious thunder and lightning, but rather in the gentle rainbow following the storm. Thank You, Holy, Gentle God. May our lives be holier and gentler this Advent season, because we, too, have been saved by Your mercy. Amen.

The Call to Abram

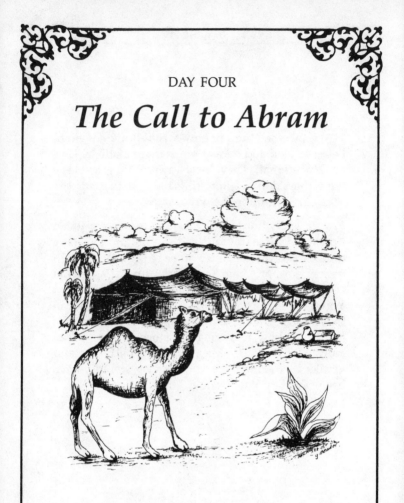

Symbol: a camel and a tent

Memory Verse: "In thee shall all families of the earth be blessed." GENESIS 12:3b

Hymns to Sing:
"I Have Decided to Follow Jesus"
"Trust and Obey"
"Leaning on the Everlasting Arms"

THE CALL TO ABRAM

(CHILDREN)

Scripture: Genesis 12:1-7

Devotion: When we think of a camel and a tent, we think of people who travel a lot. Let me tell you about a man named Abraham. God loved Abraham and told him to leave his country and relatives to go to another country that he had never seen before. That's like going to live in another house without even looking at it! You would have to really trust God, wouldn't you?

That's what Abraham did. He crossed deserts where there was no water, and he lived in tents. When Abraham got to the land, God promised him that through his family, all the world would be blessed. Let's read that verse again. (Genesis 12:3) We are so glad Abraham obeyed God, because through him, Jesus was born!

Questions:
   "What did God tell Abraham to do?"
   "Would you have been afraid to travel to a strange, faraway land?"
   "Did Abraham obey?"
   "Because of Abraham's faith, who did God promise would come from his family?" (Jesus)

Prayer: Dear Lord, we thank You that Abraham had the faith to do what You wanted him to do. Because he obeyed, You blessed him with a new land and many children. Help us to obey You in all things. Amen.

THE CALL TO ABRAM

(ADULTS)

Scriptures: Genesis 12:1-7; Hebrews 11:8, Matthew 1:1

Devotion: The belief of Abram was a mighty act of faith. Abram was called to leave his country, his relatives, and his father's home, to go to another country which he would inherit. When God spoke to Abram, he believed, and when he believed, he obeyed. Abram left the Mesopotamian Valley and came as a pilgrim and a stranger into the promised land of Canaan. Hebrews 11:8-9 states, "By faith, he sojourned in the land of promise, as in a strange country, dwelling in tabernacles with Isaac and Jacob, the heirs with him of the same promise."

What was that promise? In Genesis 17:5 God gave Abram a new name. The name Abraham means "Father of many nations." God wanted a people through whom He could work to bring salvation to the ends of the earth. The purpose of the founding of the Jewish nation was to bring forth the Lord Jesus Christ.

Prayer: You come to us in this Advent time, Yahweh, as You came to Abraham many years ago. You come to us with that same call—to be a people through whom others will be blessed. We pray that we will have that same faith to obey You in all things. Open our lives to live out Your calling. Come, Emmanuel, come. Amen.

Isaac and the Lamb

Symbol: a lamb

Memory Verse: "Behold the Lamb of God which taketh away the sin of the world." JOHN 1:29b

Thought for the Day:
> What can I give Him, poor as I am?
> If I were a shepherd, I would give Him a lamb
> If I were a Wise Man, I would do my part—
> But, what I can I give Him. Give my heart.
> *Christina Rossetti*

Hymns to Sing:
"Blessed Be the Name"
"My Faith Looks up to Thee"
"'Tis So Sweet to Trust in Jesus"

Question to Ponder: Is Jesus your Lamb?

ISAAC AND THE LAMB

(CHILDREN)

Scriptures: Genesis 22:1-13; John 1:29b

Devotion: Do you remember when God promised Abraham many people in his family? God gave Abraham a boy named Isaac, and one day God told Abraham to take Isaac to a mountain and kill him. This was a special opportunity for Abraham to show his complete trust and love in God. Abraham took a knife out to kill his son, Isaac, and then suddenly God told him to stop. He told Abraham to look in the bushes, and when he did, do you know what he found? (a lamb) God told Abraham to let the lamb take Isaac's place. Isaac lived, but the lamb had to die.

Do you know who our Lamb is? (Jesus) Let's read again in our Bible. (John 1:29) Jesus took our place on the cross, just as the lamb took Isaac's place, so we could live. He had no sin at all, but He placed our sins on Himself and died for us. Let's thank God for that right now.

Prayer: God, we thank You that You loved us enough at Christmas to give what was dearest to You, Your Son, Jesus Christ. Thank You for our Lamb, Jesus. Amen.

Questions:
   "What did God tell Abraham to do?"
   "Why did God tell him to do this?"
   "Did Isaac die? What happened?"
   "Who is our Lamb?"

ISAAC AND THE LAMB

(ADULTS)

Scriptures: Genesis 22:1-19; Isaiah 53:7; John 1:29; I Peter 1:19

Devotion: Knowing the will of God is one thing. Doing it is another. The call from God to kill Isaac was the greatest test of Abraham's mature faith. Because of Abraham's trust in the character of God, our Jehovah was able to provide an example of the Doctrine of Atonement. He was preparing the people for what Christ would one day do for them. In Chapter 22 of Genesis, we see substitutionary atonement, in which another animal takes the place of a human. The ram caught in the thicket is but a symbol of our Savior, Jesus. From this sacrifice on Mount Moriah, we see prefigured the sacrifice of the Son of God at Calvary. By his blood we are made righteous!

It is interesting to note that the place Abraham was to sacrifice Isaac (Mt. Moriah) was the exact mountain in Jerusalem where Solomon's temple was built. When Christ died on Calvary, the veil of the Temple was torn, symbolizing the final end of the sacrificial system. Today the Moslem mosque, the Dome of the Rock, is located on this site.

Prayer: Jehovah, we know You provide all things for us. Teach us to give these blessings—our health, talents, family, friends, and jobs to You when You ask for them. Thank You for a man like Abraham who trusted Your love so completely. Thank You, even more, that You gave what was dearest to You—Jesus, Your Son. Amen.

DAY SIX

Jacob's Ladder

Symbol: a ladder

Memory Verse: "Behold, I am with thee, and will keep thee in all places, whither thou goest."
GENESIS 28:15a

Hymns to Sing:

"We Are Climbing Jacob's Ladder"
"Spirit of God Descend upon My Heart"
"Have Thine Own Way, Lord"

JACOB'S LADDER
(CHILDREN)

Scripture: Genesis 28:10-17

Devotion: Have you ever had a dream? Let me tell you about a dream Jacob had. Jacob was Isaac's son. He was taking a long journey to another country to find a wife. Jacob felt very alone and very tired. He lay down on the ground, used a stone for a pillow, and went to sleep. He dreamed a strange and wonderful dream. He saw a ladder that reached way up to the sky! Angels were going up and down the ladder and God was standing at the top. Jacob was told that many wonderful things would happen to him because God loved him. From Jacob's family, Jesus would come. When Jacob awoke, he knew that God was with him and he would never be the same again!

Questions:
    "Where was Jacob going?"
    "What did he see in his dream?"
    "What did God tell him?"

Prayer: Dear Lord, sometimes we feel all alone. Help us to know that You are always there with us and will never leave us. Help our thoughts to be always on You—when we are awake or when we sleep. Amen.

JACOB'S LADDER

(ADULTS)

Scriptures: Genesis 27:41-28:22

Devotion: Jacob would not have been the person we would have chosen to continue the lineage of Jesus. He was alone, a fugitive, and a disgrace to all. He himself felt like a failure. Yet God, in His great love and tenderness, showed Jacob a ladder reaching from earth to heaven. The Lord Himself stood at the top. At the foot was a poor, helpless, and forsaken man. The ladder was a symbol that Jacob was not far from the arms of God.

The ladder is also a type or symbol of Jesus. There is now uninterrupted communion between God and man. Jesus left His glory in Heaven and descended to become a man. Because of His death, the gap between heaven and earth was bridged forever. This story shows how God used a helpless man to become the source of blessing and means of salvation to the entire world.

Prayer: Lord Jesus, it is comforting to know that You come to the most unlikely of people, asking them, as You asked Jacob, to receive Your blessing. We ask You to come to us when we are discouraged and feel like failures. May our goals and dreams be centered on glorifying You. May they not die in our minds, but cause us to work without ceasing for their attainment. We know that without Your death, we would be eternally separated from God. Thank You for providing the Way for all people. Amen.

DAY SEVEN

Joseph's Coat of Many Colors

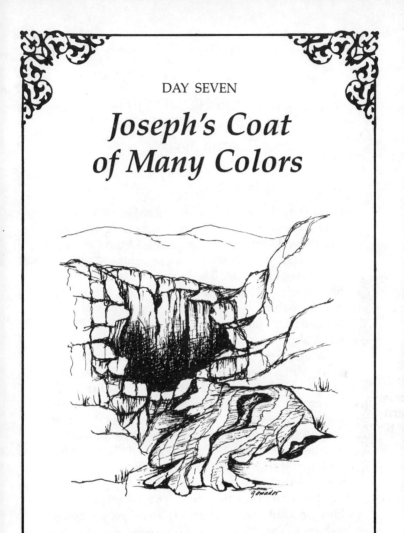

Symbol: a colorful coat

Memory Verse: "And we know that all things work together for good to them that love God."
ROMANS 8:28a

Hymns to Sing:
"Kum Ba Yah"
"If Jesus Goes with Me"
"It Is Well with My Soul"

JOSEPH'S COAT
OF MANY COLORS

(CHILDREN)

Scirptures: Genesis 37:3-36; 50:18-21; Romans 8:28

Devotion: If God loves us and takes care of us, why do troubles come? This is something we can't understand, but we have a promise from God that He will use everything (even our troubles) for our good if we love Him. The Bible gives us a wonderful example for this in the story of Joseph. He had many troubles, but all his troubles turned out for his good and for the good of many more of God's people.

Jacob loved his son Joseph very much and had given him a special coat of many colors. One day Joseph went out to find his brothers in the field. His brothers were angry and jealous because of some dreams Joseph had. The dreams seemed to say that all of Joseph's brothers would bow down before him some day. Not only that, but the beautiful coat was the kind that important people wore. It showed that their father thought Joseph was the most important of his sons. They wanted to kill him. Instead, they sold him to some people going to Egypt. This all sounds bad, doesn't it?

God allowed this to happen to Joseph for a greater purpose. Joseph became a great ruler in Egypt and when his brothers needed help, he was able to take care of them. God was with Joseph throughout all of this. Even though his brothers had been bad to him, Joseph was willing to forgive them. God wants you to forgive others, too, just as Joseph did.

Questions:
   "Who was given the coat of many colors?"
   "Who gave him the coat?" (Jacob—his name was
   changed to Israel.)
   "Did Joseph's brothers like this?"
   "What did they do?"
   "Did Joseph hurt his brothers when they hurt him?"
   "Why is it important for us to forgive others?"
   "Can you think of someone you need to forgive right
   now?" (Let's pray about it.)

Prayer: Dear God, we know You have a great plan
for each of our lives. Sometimes things happen to
us that hurt us and are bad. Help us to know that
You can change the bad things that happen to us
into good if we only trust in You. May we never
do anything that would be mean or hateful to anyone else. Amen.

JOSEPH'S COAT OF MANY COLORS

(ADULTS)

Scriptures: Genesis 37-50, especially 50:18-21;
Romans 8:28

Devotion: Because of jealousy and hatred over a
coat of many colors, Joseph's brothers conspired
against him. In 1850 B.C. Joseph was sold into slavery and taken to Egypt. We, in our human

wisdom, question these acts of cruelty. God's objective, however, was to take the children of Israel out of Canaan because of the abominations going on with the Canaanites. The sons of Jacob needed to be separated from the people of the land. Egypt was the perfect place for them because she despised the Jews and would not have anything to do with them. Therefore they would stay pure until their return to the promised land.

Chapter 38 of Genesis is the story of Judah and Tamar. Tamar is found in the genealogy of the Messiah (Matthew 1:3). This is another example of how God, in His infinite wisdom, used what seemed to be terrible circumstances to preserve His people and the lineage of Christ.

Prayer: Dear Lord, sometimes as we see the chaos and hurt in our world today, it is hard to understand Your purposes. We know that You are a sovereign Lord, however, and we are reminded of Your great promises to us that never change! Correct our mistakes and right the wrongs that we knowingly or innocently do. We bow to Your Lordship. Amen.

Moses and the Ten Commandments

Symbol: a tablet with numbers

Memory Verse: "Thy word have I hid in mine heart, that I might not sin against thee." PSALM 119:11

Hymns to Sing:
"Lord, I Want to Be a Christian"
"Come, Thou Long-Expected Jesus"
"Trust and Obey"

MOSES AND THE
TEN COMMANDMENTS

(CHILDREN)

Scriptures: Exodus 32:15-18; 20:1-20; Psalm 119:11

Devotion: How does God tell us how to live? (Bible)
The Bible tells us what we must do and not do.
Long ago, when the people of Israel were brought
out of Egypt, God gave them laws to live by. These
laws were called the Ten Commandments. God
wrote on these stones and gave the stones to a man
named Moses who had been the leader in freeing
the people from Egypt. Jesus is like Moses—freeing
us from our sins if we are willing to follow Him.

Can you name the Ten Commandments? God
tells us to love Him and to always obey Him. We
should never pray to anyone but God. It says we
should never use God's name in vain. Do you know
what that means? We should make the Sabbath
day a special day to worship Him. It says on the
stones to respect our parents and to do what they
tell us to do. Another rule is that we should not
murder anyone or take anything that does not belong to us. We should never say untrue things
about someone or lie. We should be faithful to the
one we marry, and we should never desire what
our friends have. God wants us to obey His rules
for that pleases Him!

Questions:
    "What were the laws called that were given to Moses?"
    "Can you remember one of the rules on the stones?"
    "Why does He give us these laws?"
    "Why does your family have rules for you?"

Prayer: Dear Lord, thank You for the laws that You have given us in the Bible to help us not sin. We know we will fail You, but with Your love and mercy, we will continue trying to keep them. Thank You for freeing us from our sins by Your Son's death on the Cross. Amen.

MOSES AND THE
TEN COMMANDMENTS

(ADULTS)

Scriptures: Exodus 1-15; 20; 32:15-18; Psalm 119-11; Galatians 3:19

Devotion: The whole history of the children of Israel is an example of human redemption. Man is a slave to sin. In Israel's deliverance from the slavery of Egypt, we see the redemption of our sins. The journey through the wilderness is like our journey through life as Christians. Just as God gave the Ten Commandments to keep His people on course to the Promised Land, He gives us His Word today to help us become the Spirit-controlled Christians through which He can work.

In Galatians 3:19, we read that the Law was created to bring people to Christ. We must be aware of our sin before we can see the need for salvation in Christ. The Law serves as a pattern for those striving in righteousness.

Prayer: Lord, when the children of Israel were slaves in a strange land, You sent them a leader, letting them know You are a God who cares about them. You gave them the Law to remind them of their sinfulness. We know our need for You. We fail every day. We confess these sins to You, and ask that by Your mercy You forgive us. Thank You for sending our Emancipator, Jesus, to free us from the bondage of sin. Thank You for sending Your Spirit to empower us to live a life for You. Amen.

Canaan, the Promised Land of Blessings

Symbol: a cluster of grapes

Memory Verse: "Bless the Lord, O my Soul, and forget not all his benefits." PSALM 103:2

Hymns to Sing:
   "God Is So Good"
   "On Jordan's Stormy Banks"
   "Showers of Blessings"

CANAAN,
THE PROMISED LAND
OF BLESSINGS

(CHILDREN)

Scriptures: Numbers 13:1-2, 17-23, 27; Psalm 103:2

Devotion: (Show symbol) What is this? (grapes) Have you ever seen a bunch of grapes so big and juicy that two men had to carry it? Let's read this story in the Bible. (Numbers)

Moses told twelve spies to go into the Promised Land. They found the grapes and brought them home for all their friends to see. God wanted to give His children all of these blessings, but the people were afraid to go into the land. God told them He would take care of them, but they listened to their own hearts and disobeyed. It took many years, but God was faithful in His promises. After forty more years, the children obeyed and God led them into the land of blessings.

This is the way it is in our lives. God wants to give us many good things—if we will just let Him do it. Let's go to God in prayer.

Prayer: Dear Lord, let us never take for granted the blessings You have given us. You gave us a home where our parents love us, and food and clothes. You have given us a greater blessing, however. Just as You led the children into a land of blessings, lead us into the new life You give in Your Son, Jesus Christ. Thank You for sending Him. Amen.

Question:

"Where does God want the children of Israel to go?"

"Will the people obey God and do what God says?"

"Does God want to give us blessings?"

42

CANAAN,
THE PROMISED LAND
OF BLESSINGS

(ADULTS)

Scriptures: Numbers 13-14:38; 24:17; Psalm 103:2

Devotion: After years in the wilderness, the children of God had finally reached the Promised Land. Twelve men were sent as spies into the land. After forty days, two of the men, Joshua and Caleb, reported that the land was overflowing with blessings for the people. Ten of the spies discouraged the people from obeying what God had told them to do by telling them the enemy was too powerful. The whole camp was influenced by these ten men. Instead of receiving blessings, God punished them by allowing them to wander for forty more years.

God, however, assured them that in spite of their failure, He would not abandon His people. Most of them died in the wilderness, but a remnant reached the Promised Land. Out of this remnant came a King. This did not mean only David, but the greater Son of David, Jesus Christ.

Prayer: Conquering Lord—Your blessings are waiting for us! Help us to step out, with eyes that do not see, to receive those promises of life more abundantly. We thank You for Jesus coming to earth at Bethlehem to bring us a new and better Way. Amen.

43

Ruth and Boaz

Symbol: a sheaf of wheat

Memory Verse: "Thy people shall be my people, and thy God my God." RUTH 1:16b

Hymns to Sing:
"Praise Him in the Morning"
"Some Bright Morning"
"Come Thou Almighty King"

RUTH AND BOAZ

(CHILDREN)

Scriptures: Ruth 1:16; 2:5-17; 4:14

Devotion: Let me tell you about the story of Ruth. Ruth did not know God at first and she was not from Israel. Her husband died, but she loved her mother-in-law so much she was willing to follow her to Bethlehem. There she began to love God. She wanted to take care of her mother-in-law and she worked in the wheat fields to get food for both of them to eat. This is where a man named Boaz saw her, and they were married. They had a child named Obed. One day a greater Child would come because of this marriage. Do you know His Name? (Jesus)

Questions:
"Did Ruth love her mother-in-law?"
"Did she learn to love our God?"
"Where did she meet Boaz?"
"Did she marry him?"

Prayer: Dear Lord, we thank You for Ruth. She had nothing to give except her love for her family and for You. Help us to give all our love to You. Amen.

RUTH AND BOAZ

(ADULTS)

Scriptures: Ruth 1-4; Matthew 1:5

Devotion: The story of Ruth, a Moabite woman, tells of a young girl surrendering her life to a new faith. This was a deliberate choice of a heart which belonged first of all to Naomi and then to God. Ruth's love for Naomi melted into her love for Naomi's God. Her faithfulness is made evident by her willingness to glean the fields for her family. This obedience brought Ruth and Boaz together. They conceived a son, Obed, and Ruth established her position as ancestress of David and Christ.

Boaz is symbolic of Jesus. He was a kinsman redeemer. (Ruth 4:14) Boaz was wealthy, prominent, and related to Naomi. Jesus is eternally wealthy and related to God. He is part of the Trinity which is the union of the Father, Son, and Holy Spirit in one divine nature. Boaz redeemed Ruth by marriage. Christ redeems us by His blood.

Prayer: How beautifully You provided for Ruth who loved You and Your people. Thank You that people like her, needy yet rich in Your love, are part of the lineage of the Savior. Help us to obey as Ruth did, not from obligation but love. We wait for the Redeemer to come this Advent season. Amen.

DAY ELEVEN

King David

Symbol: a slingshot

Memory Verse: "The Lord is my Shepherd; I shall not want." PSALM 23:1 (This was a song David wrote for the Lord.)

Hymns to Sing:
"Only a Boy Named David"
"I'll Go Where You Want Me to Go"
"Let All Mortal Flesh Keep Silence"
"The New 23rd"

KING DAVID

(CHILDREN)

Scriptures: I Samuel 16:1, 13; 17:1-9, 40, 45-50

Devotion: Do you know who used a slingshot to kill a great giant in the Bible? (David) Yes, it was David and he was one of the greatest kings in the world! He started out as a shepherd boy, taking care of sheep. He was strong and good, and God decided to let him be king over His people. Let's see what happens in the Bible. (Read 1 Samuel 16:1, 13) God told Samuel to pour oil over David's head so that David would know that someday he was going to be king. Can you tell me about the battle David had with Goliath while he was still a shepherd boy? Let's read the story in our Bible. (1 Samuel 17:1-9, 40, 45-50)

The giant came to fight God's people, and everyone was afraid of Him except David. David knew that God's spirit was with him and would take care of him. He didn't take a gun but a small slingshot, and with one stone Goliath was hit and fell over dead. Later David became a mighty king because he obeyed God and did the things that pleased Him, and through David, Jesus was in the family line to be our King.

Questions:
 "Who did Samuel pour oil over to be king?"
 "What was David before he was king?" (shepherd)
 "Why was David not afraid of Goliath?" (God's Spirit
  was with him)

Prayer: Jesus, we thank You for a shepherd boy named David who loved You so much he was willing to die for You. Please help us to love You with all our hearts. Even greater than King David, we thank You for Jesus, the King of our lives. Amen.

KING DAVID

(ADULTS)

Scriptures: 1 Samuel 16-17

Devotion: As we read the life of David, we realize he was a man after God's own Heart. His sins are spelled out in letters as large as his virtues. The striking difference, however, is the attitude of David. When confronted with his sin, he repented. The forgiveness of David is a reminder to us that we can find forgiveness and mercy at the hands of God. David also established the royal family to which Jesus would be born. This fulfilled the prophecy that the Savior of Israel must be of royal blood.

Prayer: God, our King, You gave David a heart of repentance. You helped him bring your people to great heights of national prosperity. Yet even this mighty king must bow before the cradle of King Jesus. Christ's kingdom reaches to all nations and knows no end. We too, in our prosperity, bow before King Jesus, in hopeful expectation of the day when every knee shall bow to Him, declaring Him Lord of all. Teach us to live now in the reality of that hope, spreading Your good news to all people. Amen.

Josiah Finds the Law

Symbol: a scroll or bible

Memory Verse: "Thy word is a lamp unto my feet, and a light unto my path." PSALM 119:105

Hymns to Sing:
"The B-I-B-L-E"
"Break Thou the Bread of Life"

JOSIAH FINDS THE LAW

(CHILDREN)

Scriptures: II Kings 23:1-3; Psalm 119:105

Devotion: Right now, God is pleased we are having these devotions! He is very pleased when we read our Bibles because the Bible is like a lamp to us. It shows us how to live and stay close to God.

Long ago there was a boy named Josiah who became the king when he was only eight years old. His father had been a wicked king and had made the people stop loving God and start worshiping idols. The people had even forgotten they had a Bible! Josiah wanted to serve God. One day, Josiah sent some men to the church to clean it up because the people had not been to church in a long time. They found the church in a mess, but they also found an old scroll.

When Josiah opened the scroll he realized that it was God's Bible that had been lost for a long time! Wouldn't that be terrible, to lose our Bible and not have it? He read that God would punish the people if they worshiped idols and not God. After the people heard this, they were sorry for their sins. They told God they would serve Him and would follow His Laws found in the Book. This pleased God very much!

Questions:

"Who was Josiah?" (a king of Judah)

"What did he find at church?" (an old scroll which was part of the Bible)

"Why does God want us to read the Bible?"

Prayer: Father, we thank Thee for Thy Law that tells us how to be happy and good. Help us to obey it just the way King Josiah did. Amen.

JOSIAH FINDS THE LAW

(ADULTS)

Scriptures: II Kings 22-23:25; Psalm 119:105

Devotion: King Josiah showed remarkable wisdom as a young man. He himself was the motivator of all the reformation acts during his reign. It was during the renovation of the temple that the long lost sacred copy of the book of the Law was found. The reading of the Law was proclaimed before all at the temple, and a spiritual renewal occurred. For a brief time, they destroyed all idols and began serving the covenantal God. This was the last united religious act before God sent Judah into captivity.

Prayer: We so often stray from Your ways, Lord. We forget the guidance You have given us in Your Work, the Bible. Call us back as You called back Your servant Josiah when he found Your Law. We know that following Your ways indeed brings life. Watch over us and call us back to discover You when we begin to lose Your way. Amen.

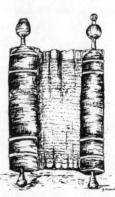

Prophecy of Shoot from the Stump of Jesse

Symbol: a stump with fresh shoot or leaf

Memory Verse: "And the Word was made flesh, and dwelt among us, and we beheld his glory." JOHN 1:14a

Hymns to Sing:
"Jesus, Name Above All Names"
"O Come, O Come Emmanuel"
"Redeeming Love"

PROPHECY OF SHOOT FROM THE STUMP OF JESSE

(CHILDREN)

Scriptures: Isaiah 11:1-5; John 1:14a

Devotion: It is from this symbol that we get the name of our tree--the Advent Jesse Tree. Do you know who Jesse was? He was the father of David, the king who established the royal family. A thousand years later, Jesus would be born into this royal line in Bethlehem. The stump represents Jesse. Do you know who the green leaf is? (Jesus) Let's read the first verse of our Bible lesson today. (Isaiah 11:1)

Questions:
   "Who is the stump?"
   "Who is the green leaf?"

Prayer: We thank You for our families who have gone on to be with You. We know they lived lives pleasing to You. Help us to live a life that would be worthy of You. Come Lord Jesus. Come and save our world. Amen.

PROPHECY OF SHOOT FROM THE STUMP OF JESSE

(ADULTS)

Scriptures: Isaiah 11:1-5, 10; John 1:14a; I Samuel 16:1-3; Revelation 5:5

Devotion: Although God had to warn His people that they would be cut off for a time because of their sins, the prophet Isaiah sang for them a new song of hope. From their brokenness would shoot forth a New Branch. Christ would be firmly planted in righteousness and justice. Through the family tree of Jesse and David, Jesus, the "Anointed One" would come. This is the literal meaning of Messiah, or Christ.

Prayer: Holy Father, we thank You for the heritage of our families. May we never forget the example of their lives. We praise You for the saints in Your Word who teach us that You alone are our Provider and Protector. We wait with Your people of ancient times, Mighty Pruner, for the flowering of Your New Branch, our Savior, Jesus Christ. Amen.

DAY FOURTEEN

Prophecy of the Lion and Lamb Resting Together

Symbol: lion and lamb

Memory Verse: "His rest shall be glorious."
ISAIAH 11:10b

Hymns to Sing:
"Doxology"
"Surely Goodness and Mercy"
"O for a Thousand Tongues to Sing"

PROPHECY OF THE LION AND LAMB RESTING TOGETHER

(CHILDREN)

Scripture: Isaiah 11:6-10

Devotion: What do you see in this symbol? (lion and lamb) Is the lion hurting the lamb? (No) Do you remember when God made the earth in the beginning? Everything was perfect! The animals lived with each other and there was peace! Everything praised Him before sin came to spoil His wonderful creation. One day our world will be like this again. The lions will lie down with the lambs, the cows will eat supper with the bears, and nothing will ever hurt His children again. God will make every creature kind and gentle. There won't be any sickness, or fighting, or death! This will all happen when Jesus comes again! When we think of all the wonderful happiness that is coming, we should pray for Him to come soon, shouldn't we? Let's do that right now!

Prayer: O Lord, we look forward to when You will come and make everything perfect in our world again. It will be a place where everything will praise You and where there will be no more sin. You are so great, and we praise You for being our King! Help us to be Your children so that we can share in Your new world. Amen.

Questions:
  "Will the lion hurt children someday?"
  "When will all this happen?"

PROPHECY OF THE LION
AND LAMB
RESTING TOGETHER

(ADULTS)

Scriptures: Isaiah 11:6-10; Matthew 25:31-46; Revelation 21:1-7; Philippians 2:9-11

Devotion: The scriptures allude to the work and future glory of the Redeemer that will be seen at His second coming. The restoration of Israel and the blessings that will come are all predicted. The scene shows that Christ will come not only as a Judge but as a Provider of Peace to the world. There will be a new heaven and earth with Christ on the throne.

Prayer: Your reign, coming Savior, will extend not only over all the nations, but over all created things. Once again, all of creation will be in complete harmony. We long for Your coming again, when there will be no more tears or pain. Come, Alpha and Omega, and create Your new heaven and earth. Amen.

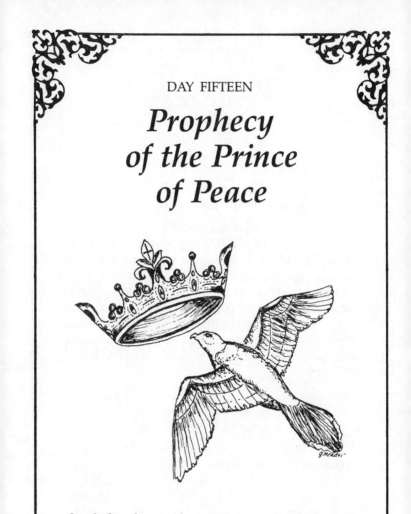

DAY FIFTEEN

Prophecy of the Prince of Peace

Symbol: a dove and crown

Memory Verse: "Peace I leave with you, my peace I give unto you: not as the world giveth, give I unto you. Let not your heart be troubled, neither let it be afraid." JOHN 14:27

Hymns to Sing:
"I've Got Peace Like a River"
"Hark the Herald Angels Sing"
"Let There Be Peace on Earth"

PROPHECY
OF THE PRINCE
OF PEACE

(CHILDREN)

Scriptures: Isaiah 9:6-7; John 14:27

Devotion: There are many names we give to describe Jesus. Can you think of any? (Savior, Light of the World, etc.) Do you know what the dove symbolizes? (Peace) What do you think of when you see a crown? (a king or prince) Another name the Bible gives Jesus is Prince of Peace. It is found in our verses today. Let's read them. (Isaiah 9:6-7) We are so glad that Jesus came teaching us to love and not to fight with others. He truly is our Prince of Peace.

Questions:
"When Jesus came did He bring an army?"
"Did Jesus live a life of love and peace?"

Prayer: Dear Lord, sometimes our friends talk about us or make fun of us, and it hurts deep inside. When we feel this way, help us to remember that You are the Prince of Peace and You can bring peace in our lives. Also help us to be like You, showing kindness and love in all things. Thank You, Jesus, for bringing peace to our world. Amen.

PROPHECY
OF THE PRINCE
OF PEACE

(ADULTS)

Scriptures: Isaiah 2:2-4; 9:2-7; John 14:27

Devotion: Long before Jesus was born, Isaiah the prophet foretold that God would send a Savior to the world. We believe Jesus fulfilled this prophecy!

Many names have been given to Jesus, and many symbols are used to convey what He means to us. This symbol reminds us that He is the Prince of Peace. He not only taught peace but lived the life of peace. One day He will establish a government of peace in which there will be no end.

Prayer: The sounds of war are all around us, Prince of Peace. We have chosen our own ways of power and force, rather than Your way of love and justice. We rejoice in You, wonderful Prince, and we wait expectantly for Your reentry into our world of war. Bring us Your peace—now and forever. Amen.

Prophecy of a Gentle Shepherd

Symbol: a lamb and a staff

Memory Verse: "My sheep hear my voice, and I know them, and they follow me." JOHN 10:27

Hymns to Sing:
"Alleluia"
"The Ninety and Nine"
"Savior, Like a Shepherd Lead Us"

PROPHECY OF A GENTLE SHEPHERD

(CHILDREN)

Scriptures: Isaiah 40:11; Psalm 23:1, 2; John 10:27

Devotion: Do you remember King David, who was once a shepherd boy? He took great care of his sheep and even killed a lion and a bear to protect them! David wrote a song about how the Lord was a good shepherd to him. Can you remember that memory verse? (Psalm 23:1, from Day Eleven of devotions)

The Lord is our Shepherd, always watching over us and protecting us! He never sleeps, and He knows each one of us by our name. He can even look inside our hearts to know if we really believe in Him or not!

If you love and trust Him, you are His sheep. When you hear His voice, you will follow Him in every way. You will know that He will take care of you!

Questions:
   "Do sheep need a shepherd? Why?"
   "Who is our Shepherd?"
   "Are we lost without Him?"

Prayer: Gentle Shepherd, we know we would be lost without You. Thank You for always being there, patiently guiding us back into Your loving arms. May we always listen to hear Your voice and follow Your call. Amen.

PROPHECY OF A
GENTLE SHEPHERD

(ADULTS)

Scriptures: Isaiah 40:9-11;   Psalm 23;   John 10:27; John 10:11-16

Devotion: The prophets had predicted that the true Shepherd would come to gather and restore the lost sheep. Christ came into the world calling to His own. Those who hear His voice, draw close to Him.

There are so many joys and benefits involved when we let Christ be our Shepherd. He comes to us calling to take us under His care. The choice is ours. He longs to lead us through this perilous journey called life. He wants us to know Him in the most personal way. To follow Christ means we become identified with His plan and purpose for our lives. His standards and values become ours. His life becomes our life. If we are in Him, we will have His peace of serenity, strength, and stability at all times.

Prayer: Gentle Shepherd, "all we like sheep have gone astray; we have turned every one to his own way." We need Your tender care. May we be receptive to Your loving arms and follow where You gently lead us. Amen.

Prophecy of the Suffering Servant

Symbol: a cross

Memory Verse: "I lay down my life for the sheep."
JOHN 10:15

Hymns to Sing:
"The Old Rugged Cross"
"When I Survey the Wondrous Cross"
"What Wondrous Love Is This"

PROPHECY OF THE SUFFERING SERVANT

(CHILDREN)

Scriptures: Isaiah 53; Luke 2:8-18; John 19:11-18; John 10:15

Devotion: Did you know that God is pure and holy and cannot be a part of sin? We can see this by comparing ourselves to a new shirt. What does the new shirt look like? What happens when we get dirt on it? The dirt is like the sin in our lives making us unclean. Is this the way God is? No, He is perfect and spotless and He will allow no sin to touch Him! That is why He would not talk or be with us anymore until the dirt or sin in our lives was gone.

God, however, did not want to be away from us. He planned for Someone pure to wash our sins away and bring us back to Him forever! Do you know who that Someone was? Jesus took all our sins on Himself and died on the cross so our sins could be forgiven. He was willing for the people to put nails in His hands and feet because that was the way to nail our sins to the cross. He loved us so much that He was willing to die for us even when we were unclean and had sin in our hearts. He gave His life so that we could have life forevermore!

> Children, can you tell me why
> Jesus came to bleed and die?
> He was happy high above,
> Dwelling in His Father's love,
> Yet He left His joy and bliss,
> For a wicked world like this.

We were all by sin undone,
Yet He loved us ev'ry one;
So to earth He kindly came,
On the cross to bear our shame,
And to wash away our guilt
In the precious blood He spilt.
                    —*author unknown*

Questions:
   "Why did Jesus come to earth?"
   "Were people mean to Jesus?"
   "Is Jesus your Savior?"

Prayer: Dear Lord Jesus, how can we ever thank You enough for giving us You at Christmas time. Thank You for dying on the cross for us. Help us to show our love by believing in You and living for You. We sing Your praises as the angels did on Christmas night. Amen.

PROPHECY OF THE SUFFERING SERVANT

(ADULTS)

Scriptures: Isaiah 53; John 19:11-18; John 10:15; Matthew 26:28; Hebrews 9:22; Romans 5:9, 10, and I Peter 1:1, 19

Devotion: As we look to the cross we realize that this is the reason Christ came—not only as a Sovereign but as a Savior. He wears a crown, but He also bears a cross. Without the cross, there would be no Christmas. Without Calvary, there would be no cause to celebrate the manger at Bethlehem.

Prayer: We have been waiting for Your triumphant coming, mighty God, and now we hear that You will come in sorrow and humility. These words are hard for us to understand - why the Son of God should have to suffer and die for sins You did not commit. We bow before Thee in humiliation that You would love us enough to do this for us. We are so undeserving of this gift of salvation. We are silent and awed as the shadow of Your cross falls over Your manger bed. Help us not let Your gift be in vain. May we take up Your cross and become servants, giving of ourselves to others as You gave Yourself to us, wounded and bruised for our sins. Amen.

Words to Ponder

Little baby in a manger,
You came to earth a tiny stranger,
But soon the world would know
You'd give the greatest gift of love.

You came to earth to die on Calvary
Bear the pain and shame to die for me.
I can't believe it - but it's so.

For you gave up your throne in glory.
All the pow'r of the world was in your hands.
You gave up your right to be ruler,
You gave it up—to Just Be A Man.

Your kingdom was not to be worldly,
Even tho' you could reign throughout the land.
Your glory grew dim as a baby, and it was all a
part of God's PLAN.

Little baby in a manger,
You came to earth a tiny stranger.
I found a home for you today,
Come in my heart and always stay.

Dean Lambert

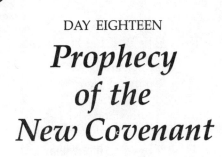

DAY EIGHTEEN

Prophecy of the New Covenant

"The Lord saith... *"I will put my law within them, and write it in their hearts."* Jer. 31:33a

Symbol: a heart with writing on it

Memory Verse: "I will put my law within them, and write it in their hearts." JEREMIAH 31:33a

Hymns to Sing:
 "Into My Heart"
 "Tell Me the Story of Jesus"

PROPHECY OF THE NEW COVENANT

(CHILDREN)

Scriptures: Jeremiah 31:31-34; Acts 16:31

Devotion: Even if Jesus is in our hearts, do we still do bad things? A long time ago, God had made a promise or a covenant with the children of Israel. As long as they obeyed His Ten Commandments, He provided for them, but if they broke any laws He punished them. Can you imagine every time you gave a dirty look to your sisters or brothers or mother and daddy, God would turn His back on You? That would be hard to live by, wouldn't it?

God saw the people continue to break His laws. In spite of all their sins, He still loved them. He decided to give them a new promise, or a New Covenant. He would write His law on their hearts. Do you know what that means?

God sent His Son Jesus Christ to earth to save us from our sins. If we ask Jesus into our hearts, He will forgive all the bad things we do. Let's read this in the Bible. (Acts 16:31) Aren't we glad we are under this New Covenant?

Questions:
    "What is a covenant?"
    "What was the Old Covenant?"
    "What is the New Covenant?"
    "Do you have Jesus written on your heart?"

Prayer: Dear God, we ask You to write Your New Law on our hearts. May Jesus come in and take away all our sins. We know that His Love can overcome any wrong we do. We praise You for providing a Way for us to be clean and holy again. Amen.

PROPHECY OF THE NEW COVENANT

(ADULTS)

Scriptures: Jeremiah 31:31-34; Deuteronomy 6:6-7; Hebrews 8-10

Devotion: Here is the prophecy that was fulfilled by Christ as our New Covenant. The old covenant was the "contract" God made with His people through giving the Law. We have seen how the people broke their side of the covenant; that is, they broke the Law.

Laws may compel obedience through a system of rewards and punishments, but something more is necessary to change man himself. The New Covenant is that "something more." Christ does not merely invite us into the kingdom of God. He brings us into the kingdom. Now we may live, not by the coercion of the laws but by "the law written upon our hearts."

"What is the relationship between the Old and the New Testaments?"

"How is the Law written upon our hearts?" (Hebrews 8-10)

Prayer: Even when the children of Israel failed You over and over, Lord, You gave them the comforting word that You were not forsaking them but rather preparing them for a New Covenant to come. We pray for the day when the Law of Jesus is indeed in all our hearts. "O Come, O Come, Emmanuel, and ransom captive Israel, that mourns in lonely exile here." Amen.

DAY NINETEEN

Prophecy of Bethlehem

Symbol: a Bethlehem town silhouette with star

Memory Verse: "I can do all things through Christ which strengtheneth me." PHILIPPIANS 4:13

Hymns to Sing:
"O Little Town of Bethlehem"
"O Come, All Ye Faithful"

PROPHECY OF BETHLEHEM

(CHILDREN)

Scripture: Luke 2:4-7

Devotion: Do you know what this symbol shows? It is the town of Bethlehem. It was a very small town and was not a very important city, but God chose it to be the place where the greatest man in the world would be born. Do you know what His name was? (Jesus)

Let's read in the Bible again about the Christmas story. (Luke 2:4-7) You might not think you can do much for God because you are small, but God can do anything in you , if you let Him.

Questions:
   "What town was Jesus born in?"
   "Was it a large or small town?"
   "Can God use you, even if you're small?"

Prayer: Dear Lord, thank You for loving all Your creatures, great and small. Just like the town of Bethlehem, we know we are small too. But if we let You, we know You can do great things in us. Lord, come into our lives. Amen.

PROPHECY OF BETHLEHEM

(ADULTS)

Scriptures: Micah 5:2-4; Luke 2:1-7

Devotion: This is the passage the chief priests and scribes quoted to King Herod when he demanded to know where the Christ Child would be born. (Matthew 2:4-6) Not only does this announce His birthplace, but it describes Him as being from the lineage of David. He is more than a descendant, however, for His "goings forth are from long ago, from the days of eternity." Christ's deity, as well as His humanity, are fully revealed from the smallest of towns, Bethlehem.

Prayer: Dear Lord, once again, we cannot begin to understand Your ways. We praise You that the awesome event of the birth of Your Son would take place in a small, insignificant town. We humbly see how You can use us to do glorious things for Thee. Just as in Bethlehem, choose us in our weakness and smallness to give rebirth to the life of Your Son. We wait His coming—to Bethlehem—and to us. Amen.

DAY TWENTY
The Exile

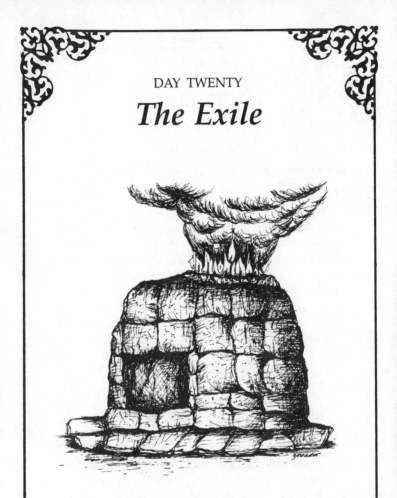

Symbol: a fiery furnace

Memory Verse: "Do not be afraid of their faces, for I am with thee to deliver thee." JEREMIAH 1:8

Hymns to Sing:
  "Three Good Men"
  "He Leadeth Me"
  "Lord Jesus I Love Thee"

THE EXILE

(CHILDREN)

Scriptures: Daniel 3: 19-29; Jeremiah 1:8

Devotion: Do you know what you must say if someone tells you to do something wrong? You must say "No"! One day, long ago, a wicked king made a great big idol or statue. And if his subjects didn't bow to it, they would be thrown into a fiery furnace or oven. When the trumpets blew, everyone bowed down except three men. Do you know their names? (Shadrach, Meshach, and Abednego) They were brave, young men. They dared to say "no" to the king, and they were willing to die for their beliefs. Do you know what happened to them? The king did throw them into the furnace, but something strange happened! Let's read our scripture. (Daniel 3:19-23)

Did they burn up? Let's read on. (Daniel 3:24-29) The king saw a fourth person in the fire walking, and it was like the Son of God. The fire did not harm them at all! Because they said no, the king began to praise God. They knew their God would deliver them from the fiery furnace, and we know God will take care of us too!

Questions:
"What were the three men's names?"
"What did the king want them to do?"
"What happened when they said no?"
"Did God take care of them?"

Prayer: Lord Jesus, sometimes we are tempted to do bad things. Help us to say no. Make us strong like Shadrach, Meshach, and Abednego to stand up and be counted for You. Help us realize that You came to always be with us and to help us in everything. Amen.

THE EXILE

(ADULTS)

Scriptures: II Kings 17:1-23; 25:1-17; Daniel 3; Isaiah 43:2; Jeremiah 1:8

Devotion: The first deportation of Judah was in 605 B.C. by the Babylonians. We see the sovereignty of God in how a "godly remnant" of the tribe of Judah was taken into captivity to preserve the lineage of His people. Through this remnant, Christ, our Supreme Judge, would come.

Idol worship was one of the main reasons God had brought judgment on the children of Israel. It is comforting to see these three Hebrew men taking a stand not to bow down to any except the Lord God. Verses 17 and 18 of Daniel 3 show the faith and courage of these men.

Prayer: Abide with us today as You did with Your people when they were strangers in a foreign land. May we, as did the three courageous men in Babylon, worship You alone. Help us to know that Your presence is always with us, even when we are rejected and hurt by those around us. We pray for Your coming. Amen.

The Return to the Land

Symbol: a brick wall

Memory Verse: "Surely I come quickly: Amen. Even so, come, Lord Jesus." REVELATION 22:20

Hymns to Sing:
"Lift up Your Heads, Ye Mighty Gates"

THE RETURN TO THE LAND

(CHILDREN)

Scriptures: Nehemiah 1:3; 2:18; 6:15, 16; Malachi 3:1; Revelation 22:20

Devotion: Do you know what this brick wall is a symbol of? It represents the Wall of Jerusalem. There was a wall that circled the whole city of Jerusalem. Do you remember how the people of Israel would never do what God wanted them to do? Because they disobeyed, God punished them by letting bad armies tear down the Wall of Jerusalem, and all the people were taken as slaves into different lands.

In order for Jesus to be born, the Bible said the people would return to Jerusalem, and sure enough, more than 400 years before Jesus was born, they began rebuilding the Wall of Jerusalem. Let's read our scripture today. When the Wall was complete, the waiting for the Messiah began. It took many years for the people to be ready for Him. Are we ready for Jesus to come to us this Christmas?

Questions:
   "What does the symbol represent?"
   "What happened to the Wall?"
   "Did the children of Israel rebuild the Wall before Jesus came to earth?"

Prayer: Dear Lord, just as the people returned to Jerusalem and began waiting for the Messiah, may we prepare our hearts for you to come this Christmas. Come, Lord Jesus, come. Amen.

THE RETURN TO THE LAND

(ADULTS)

Scriptures: Ezra 1; Nehemiah 6:15, 16; Malachi 3:1; Revelation 22:20 (For all the events of the rebuilding of the Wall, read the entire Books of Ezra and Nehemiah)

Devotion: The Book of Ezra records the fulfillment of God's promise to Judah to bring them back to their land after 70 years of captivity. After their return, the second Temple was completed under Zerubbabel, and true worship was restored in Jerusalem in 486 B.C. The Wall of Jerusalem was completed under Nehemiah's leadership in 435 B.C.

After the prophecy found in Malachi 3:1, there was silence from the prophets for 400 years. The people waited for the Messenger of the New Covenant to come. This is also quoted in Matthew 11:10; Mark 1:2; Luke 1:76; 7:27. This prophecy was fulfilled in John the Baptist as the herald of Christ's first coming.

Prayer: The time is getting ripe—the place is being readied. As Your people returned to their native land and began waiting, so may our hearts and lives be readied for Your soon arrival. Come quickly, Lord Jesus. Amen.

Words to Ponder: His Love . . .Reaching

Right from the beginning God's love has reached, and from the beginning man has refused to understand. But love went on reaching, offering itself. Love offered the eternal . . . we wanted the immediate. Love offered deep joy . . . we wanted thrills. Love offered freedom . . . we wanted license. Love offered communion with God Himself . . . we wanted to worship at the shrine of our own minds. Love offered peace . . . we wanted approval for our wars. Even yet, love went on reaching. And still today, after two thousand years, patiently, lovingly, Christ is reaching out to us today. Right through the chaos of our world, through the confusion of our minds. He is reaching . . . longing to share with us . . . the very being of God.

His love still is longing. His love still is reaching, right past the shackles of my mind. And the Word of the Father became Mary's little Son. And His love reached all the way to where I was.

Gloria Gaither

81

DAY TWENTY-TWO

The Star

Symbol: a star

Memory Verse: "When they saw the star, they rejoiced with exceeding great joy." MATTHEW 2:10

Hymns to Sing:
"Everybody Ought to Know"
"There's a Song in the Air"
"As with Gladness Men of Old"
"The Star Carol"

THE STAR

(CHILDREN)

Scriptures: Matthew 2:1-12; Revelation 22:16

Devotion: Isn't it fun to look at the stars at night? Stars are like lights, and sometimes people follow the stars to find their way home. Do you remember who followed the star at Christmas time? Let's read about it in the Bible. (Matthew 2:1-12) Isn't that a good story? Let me read verse 10 again. (v.10) Why were the wise men so happy? For many years they had studied the stars, waiting for a special star to appear. It would tell of the birth of a new King, a great King above all other kings. So when the star appeared, the wise men were very excited! They knew they would have to travel many months, but that did not bother them. When they saw Him in a house in Bethlehem, they fell down and worshiped Him and gave Him gifts.

Just as the star led the wise men to Jesus, we can find our home in Him! He is our Morning Star!

Questions:
"What did the wise men follow?"
"Why did the wise men travel so far to see this Child?"
"Who is our Morning Star?" (Revelation 22:16)
"What can we give to Jesus?"

Prayer: Dear Lord, how long the wise men must have waited to see the sign of the star! May we be able to see with our eyes Your Shining Star and find our home in You! Amen.

Words to Ponder

The wise may bring their learning,
The rich may bring their wealth,
And some may bring their greatness,
And some their strength and health;
We too would bring our treasures
To offer to the King;
We have no wealth or learning:
What shall we children bring?
We'll bring Him hearts that love Him;
We'll bring Him thankful praise,
And young souls meekly striving
To walk in holy ways:
And these shall be the treasures
We offer to the King,
And these are gifts that even
The poorest child may bring.

—author unknown

THE STAR

(ADULTS)

Scriptures: Matthew 2:1-12; Numbers 24:17; Revelation 22:16; II Peter 1:19

Devotion: The five-pointed star is called the Epiphany Star, symbolizing the body of Jesus Christ. The five points represent His hands and feet that were nailed to the Cross and His head with the crown of thorns. The Christmas story means nothing unless we, as were the wise men, are willing to search for Him. Once we find Him, we must come into Him and worship Him. As He gave the greatest gift of all to us, the gift of eternal life, we must be willing to give our lives to live for Him.

Prayer: We thank You for the example of these magi patiently and faithfully believing in the sign of the star. May we be willing to follow You, wherever You lead us. May we look forward to Your future coming to rule us as we celebrate Your first coming. Amen.

On This Day Earth Shall Ring

On this day earth shall ring
with the song children sing
to the Lord, Christ our King,
born on earth to save us;
him the Father gave us.

God's bright star, o'er his head,
Wise Men three to him led;
kneel they low by his bed,
lay their gifts before him,
praise him and adore him.

Piae Cantiones, 1582; trans. by Jane M. Joseph

DAY TWENTY-THREE

The Light of the World

Symbol: a candle or light

Memory Verse: "I am the light of the world: he that followeth me shall not walk in the darkness, but shall have the light of life." JOHN 8:12

Hymns to Sing:
"This Little Light of Mine"
"Light of the World We Hail Thee"
"Silent Night"

THE LIGHT OF THE WORLD

(CHILDREN)

Scriptures: Luke 1:26-38; 2:32; John 8:12

Devotion: The time had come for the Light of the world to be born. Do you know who the Light of the world is? The Bible says that when the angel came to Mary to tell her she would give birth to Jesus, she broke forth into a song praising God for His goodness! The True Light was finally coming into the world!

After His birth, Mary and Joseph took Jesus to church to present Him to the Lord. Simeon presented Him to the World as the "Light and Glory to all people." (Luke 2:23)

While Jesus was living in the world, He was the Light of the world. Now He has gone back to heaven, and we who trust in Him must become the lights of the world. We must always let our lights shine so that others can see Christ in us. The Lord wants us to shine for Him, like a city on top of a hill where it can always be seen. Are we happy God chooses us to shine for Him?

Questions:
   "Who was Jesus' mother?"
   "Was she willing to do what God said?"
   "Who is the Light of the world?"
   "Will you be a light for Him?"

Prayer: Dear Father in heaven, we thank You for sending us Jesus, the Light of the world, to show us what we do wrong and how to find eternal life. We want to be Jesus' lights to shine for Him. Help us to shine for Him today, like little candles burning in the night, so that someday we may shine in glory with Him. Amen.

THE LIGHT OF THE WORLD

(ADULTS)

Scriptures: Luke 1:26-56; 2:21-33; John 1:4-9;
II Corinthians 4:6; Isaiah 42:6; John 8:12; Revelation
21:23, 24; Isaiah 60:1, 3

Devotion: The time was come for the prophecies of old to be fulfilled. God's promise to send the Savior is about to occur. As Isaiah had said, "The Lord himself will give you a sign: Behold, a virgin shall conceive, and bear a son, and shall call his name Immanuel" (Isaiah 7:14). The word Immanuel is translated as meaning "God with us." When Mary heard the news from the angel, she broke forth in one of the most beautiful songs ever written, the *Magnificat.* She eagerly awaited the coming of the Light of the world. May we follow her example and be willing to let God use us in His glorious purposes. May we let His Light shine through us!

Prayer: As the time for Your coming draws near, prepare our hearts and lives. We are waiting excitedly for the Light of the world. Help us to let our lights shine for others. We also pray that You bring forth the dark corners of our hearts into Pure Light, so that we may live a more holy way. Amen.

DAY TWENTY-FOUR

Angels Proclaiming the Coming of Christ

Symbol: an angel

Memory Verse: "Glory to God in the highest, and on earth peace, good will toward men"
LUKE 2:14

Hymns to Sing:
"All Night, All Day"
"It Came upon a Midnight Clear"
"The First Noel"

ANGELS PROCLAIMING THE COMING OF CHRIST

(CHILDREN)

Scriptures: Hebrews 1:14; Luke 2:8-14; Romans 6:23

Devotion: Do you know what an angel is? An angel is a special messenger or servant. God's angels do whatever He tells them to do, and they go wherever He sends them. They bring special messages to people from God.

Can you tell me what happened to the shepherds on Christmas night? The shepherds were in the field watching over their sheep, when an angel suddenly appeared before them. The angel was bringing the greatest message of all time to them from God. Let's read about this in the Bible. (Luke 2:8-11)

Remember we have been talking about God sending a Savior? The angel and a whole sky full of angels came that Christmas night to say the Savior had finally come to the world! The angels began praising God and saying, "Glory to God in the highest, and on earth peace, good will to men." (Luke 2:14) Aren't we glad the angels brought this message to us?

Questions:
"What is an angel?"
"What was the good news the angel brought?"
"Were the angels happy that Christmas night? Why?"

Prayer: Dear Father, how can we ever thank You enough for Your great gift to us at Christmastime! We thank You for Your Son, Jesus, who loved us enough to die for us on the cross. We thank Thee for Your servants, the angels. Help us to be happy serving You too, and to sing praises as the angels did. Amen.

ANGELS PROCLAIMING THE COMING OF CHRIST

(ADULTS)

Scriptures: Luke 2:8-14; Hebrews 1:1-14; Psalm 91:11

Devotion: The thought of an angel conjures up a variety of images in our minds. An angel, however, is a messenger or a servant, and usually the message is good news.

"Peace on Earth." This is God's Christmas greeting to us. In the beautiful story of Jesus' birth, it was sung by a chorus of angelic voices. Although the shepherds were the first to hear this glorious message, it is a message for the whole world to hear today! On each Christmas Day, God repeats His greeting.

Prayer: We sing praises to You Heavenly Lord for the wonderful message You have brought. You, who made all the heaven and earth, have now given us the greatest gift of all—Your Son. Thank You for bringing us back to You by His blood. Amen.

DAY TWENTY-FIVE

The Birth of Jesus

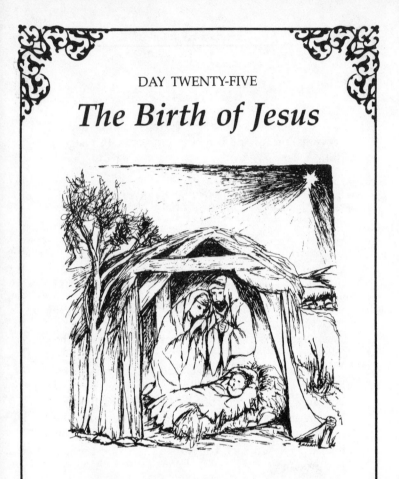

Symbol: a baby in a manger or a nativity scene

Memory Verse: "For God so loved the world, that he gave his only begotten Son, that whosoever believeth in him should not perish, but have eternal life." JOHN 3:16

Hymns to Sing:
"Away in a Manger"
"Joy to the World"
"Go Tell It on the Mountain"
"Happy Birthday"

THE BIRTH OF JESUS

(CHILDREN)

Scriptures: Luke 2:1-10; John 3:16-17

Devotion: Do you know what happens today on Christmas Day? (Show symbol) Yes, it is the day we celebrate Jesus' birthday, when He became a little baby. Jesus is different from us, however, because He was God's only Son. In fact, He was alive when the world was created. He has been from the beginning of time, just as our Advent Jesse Tree devotion said on the first day!

Can you tell me how sin came to the earth and spoiled it? God needed Someone to come to our earth and take away that sin. Jesus, the Son of God, was willing to come and be our Savior. That's why the angels sang so gloriously on that first Christmas Day—because Jesus had come to take away the sins of the world!

Jesus was willing to leave His throne in Heaven and all of His Glory to become a little baby for us. Let's read the story from the Bible. (Luke 2:1-20) Do you remember where they laid Him? They laid Him in a manger, a feeding place for the animals because no one had made room for Him.

The story of Jesus' birth is the most wonderful story in the Bible. It can be the most wonderful story for you if you make room for Him. All you have to do is to believe in Him, ask Him to come and take over your life, and He will. Isn't He wonderful?

Questions:
  "Was Jesus alive before He became a baby?" (in Heaven)
  "Who was Jesus?" (Son of God)
  "Why did Jesus come to earth?"
  "How can we make room for Him in our hearts?"

Prayer: Dear Jesus, Christmas Day is such a special day because You were born on earth! We thank You for coming as a little baby to be our Savior. Help us to make room for You in our hearts, this blessed Christmas morn. Amen.

THE BIRTH OF JESUS

(ADULTS)

Scriptures: Luke 2; 19:10; John 3:16, 17; II Corinthians 8:9

Devotion: We yearn, our Father, for the simple beauty of Christmas—for all the old familiar melodies and words that remind us of that great miracle, when He who made all things was one night to come as a Babe, to lie in the crook of a woman's arm.

Before such mystery we kneel, as we follow the shepherds and wise men to bring Thee the gift of our love--a love that we confess has not always been as warm or sincere or real as it should have been. But now, on this Christmas Day, that love would find its Beloved, and from Thee receive the grace to make it pure again, warm and real.

We bring Thee our gratitude for every token of Thy love.

—*Peter Marshall*

Prayer: Welcome, Jesus—King of our hearts—King of the universe! Overwhelm us today with Your coming and Your presence, that we may never be the same. Welcome to our home, Prince of Peace! Amen.

About the Author

Dean Meador Lambert was born, raised, and educated in Hattiesburg, Mississippi. She attended the University of Southern Mississippi where she graduated in 1974 with highest honors and a Bachelor's degree in Music Education. She has been a school music teacher and for the past fifteen years has served in various positions in the church. She is currently director of children's music and activities at Heritage United Methodist Church in Hattiesburg, to which this book is dedicated. Dean has written several Christian musicals, plays, and curriculum programs for her church.

Her most important job is as a wife and a mother to her children. She and her husband, Rick, have three daughters, Elizabeth, Emily, and Erin.

About the Illustrator

Ginger Jones Meador is a teacher and an artist. She graduated from the University of Southern Mississippi with a Bachelor's degree in Library Science. After beginning her career on the college/university level as a librarian, she chose being a full-time mommy for several years. For the past ten years, she has been teaching in both private and public-school kindergartens. She has always been an artist in her leisure time.

In response to the encouragement of her family and friends, she is currently enjoying exhibiting her work. Her lifelong skills in pen and ink and her new interest in watercolor painting have produced work receiving both placement and purchase awards in several art shows. She has a watercolor print in circulation, and has illustrated a collection of note-cards.

The Meador family, Ginger and John and children Betsy and Chuck, make their home in Hattiesburg, Mississippi, where they are members of Heritage United Methodist Church.